SPEAKI

MARR

SPEAKING
of
MARRIAGE

Irreverent Thoughts on Matrimony

Edited by
Tina & Robert Reed

A Perigee Book

A Perigee Book
Published by The Berkley Publishing Group
200 Madison Avenue
New York, NY 10016

Copyright © 1995 by Robert R. McCord & Associates, Inc.

Book design by Richard Oriolo

Cover design by Dale Fiorillo.

First edition: June 1995

Published simultaneously in Canada.

Library of Congress Cataloging-in-Publication Data

Speaking of marriage : irreverent thoughts on matrimony / edited
by Tina Reed and Robert Reed.—1st ed.
p.   cm.
"A Perigee book."
ISBN 0–399–51941–6 (alk. paper : pbk.)
1. Marriage—Quotations, maxims, etc.   2. Quotations, English.
3. Quotations.   I. Reed, Tina.   II. Reed, Robert.
PN6084.M3S64   1995
808.88'2—dc20   94-39474
                                             CIP

Printed in the United States of America

10 9 8 7 6 5 4 3 2 1

*O*nce again, the editors wish to thank
Bertha, David, Bob and Nancy.

PREFACE

Since time immemorial, wits and sages have turned sharp eyes and even sharper tongues on the ancient and honored institution of matrimony. Some have commented on the inherent contradiction in the term "wedded bliss." Others note the complications of "togetherness." And others reflect on the delicate balancing act required in a "union of equals."

Even the most happily married of men and women have stopped to ponder the ups and downs, the compromises, the trials and tribulations that inevitably accompany the merging of two individuals into one family unit. Marriage begins in a ritual—after that, we're on our own to breathe life into the institution.

Whether you are about to be wed or are celebrating an anniversary, we hope the perspectives found in this book, acerbic or wry, fond or contemplative, will bring a smile to your face, a nod of recognition or a momentary insight. Nobody said it would be easy.

TINA AND ROBERT REED

SPEAKING OF
MARRIAGE

*M*arriage, *n.* The state or condition of a community consisting of a master, a mistress and two slaves, making in all, two.

Ambrose Bierce

*M*arrying a man is like buying something you've been admiring for a long time in a shop window. You may love it when you get it home, but it doesn't always go with everything else in the house.

Jean Kerr

To keep your marriage brimming
With love in the marriage cup,
Whenever you're wrong, admit it;
Whenever you're right, shut up.

Ogden Nash

By all means marry: if you get a good wife you'll become happy; if you get a bad one, you'll become a philosopher.

Socrates

I never married because I have three pets at home that answer the same purpose as a husband. I have a dog that growls every morning, a parrot that swears all afternoon, and a cat that comes home late at night.

Marie Corelli

$\mathcal{D}$o you think your mother and I should have lived comfortably so long together if ever we had been married?

John Gay

$\mathcal{T}$he fact that one is married by no means proves that one is a mature person.

Clara Thompson

$\mathcal{A}$ lady of forty-seven who has been married twenty-seven years and has six children knows what love really is and once described it for me like this: "Love is what you've been through with somebody."

James Thurber

$\mathcal{T}$he concept of two people living together for 25 years without having a cross word suggests a lack of spirit only to be admired in sheep.

A. P. Herbert

*T*here isn't a wife in the world who has not taken the exact measure of her husband, weighed him and settled him in her own mind, and knows him as well as if she had ordered him after designs and specifications of her own.

Charles Dudley Warner

I'd rather marry a wise old man than a young fool.

Anna Maria of Braunschweig

A man likes his wife to be just clever enough to comprehend his cleverness, and just stupid enough to admire it.

Israel Zangwill

Q. Should a woman have secrets she keeps from the man she loves?

A. Should chocolates have cherry centers? Should satin pillows have fluffy stuffing?

Miss Piggy (as told to Henry Beard)

*N*o man should have a secret from his wife; she invariably finds it out.

Oscar Wilde

A husband should tell his wife everything that he is sure she will find out, and before anyone else does.

Sir Thomas Robert Dewar

*T*he good Husband keeps his Wife in the wholesome ignorance of unnecessary Secrets.

Sir Richard Steele

*A*n archeologist is the best husband a woman can have; the older she gets, the more interested he is in her.

Agatha Christie

Some people ask the secret of our long marriage. We take time to go to a restaurant two times a week. A little candlelight, dinner, soft music and dancing. She goes Tuesdays, I go Fridays.

Henny Youngman

Miss Manners agrees that it would be odd for a couple to agree on everything. Not unhealthy, just odd. The fondest of couples may disagree on nearly everything.

Judith Martin (Miss Manners)

Whatever you may look like, marry a man your own age—as your beauty fades, so will his eyesight.

Phyllis Diller

Marriage is one long conversation, chequered by disputes.

Robert Louis Stevenson

A married couple are well suited when both partners usually feel the need for a quarrel at the same time.

Jean Rostand

The best part of married life is the fights. The rest is merely so-so.

Thornton Wilder

Only two things are necessary to keep one's wife happy. One is to let her think she is having her own way, and the other, to let her have it.

  Lyndon B. Johnson

$\mathscr{A}$ wise woman will always let her husband have her way.

  Richard Brinsley Sheridan

It is true, that all married men have their own way, but the trouble is they don't all have their own way of having it!

  Artemus Ward

*B*ride, *n.* A woman with a fine prospect of happiness behind her.

Ambrose Bierce

*H*usband, *n.* One who, having dined, is charged with the care of the plate.

Ambrose Bierce

*W*edding, *n.* A ceremony at which two persons undertake to become one, one undertakes to become nothing, and nothing undertakes to become supportable.

Ambrose Bierce

*H*oneymoon: The time during which the bride believes the bridegroom's word of honor.

H. L. Mencken

*W*hen Orpheus went down to the regions below,
  Which men are forbidden to see,
He tuned up his lyre, as old histories show,
  To set his Eurydice free.

All hell was astonished a person so wise
  Should rashly endanger his life,
And venture so far—but how vast their surprise
  When they heard that he came for his wife.

Thomas Lisle

*A*n ideal wife is any woman who has an ideal husband.

Booth Tarkington

I am not in favour of long engagements. They give people the opportunity of finding out each other's character before marriage, which I think is never advisable.

Oscar Wilde

*I*f I ever marry it will be on a sudden impulse, as a man shoots himself.

H. L. Mencken

*A*s the bride in the newspaper account told the police the other day after she shot her new husband at their wedding reception, "No marriage is perfect."

Erma Bombeck

*O*ne advantage of marriage, it seems to me, is that when you fall out of love with him, or he falls out of love with you, it keeps you together until you maybe fall in again.

Judith Viorst

*T*he critical period in matrimony is breakfast-time.

A. P. Herbert

*L*ove is a wonderful thing and highly desirable in marriage.

Rupert Hughes

*W*oman wants monogamy;
Man delights in novelty. . . .
With this the gist and sum of it,
What earthly good can come of it?

Dorothy Parker

*M*aybe today's successful marriage is when a man is in love with his wife and only one other woman.

Matt Basile

Every good wife should commit a few infidelities to keep her husband in countenance.

George Bernard Shaw

We got married because we didn't know one another well enough to live together.

Erma Bombeck

*T*here is not one in a hundred of either sex who is not taken in when they marry. . . . It is, of all transactions, the one in which people expect most from others, and are least honest themselves.

Jane Austen

*M*arriage often unites for life two people who scarcely know each other.

Honoré de Balzac

*G*et married, but never to a man who is home all day.

George Bernard Shaw

Another vacation this year? You bet. We're firm believers that at least once a year a family ought to get away from it all so they can appreciate good food, plush lodgings, convenient stores, and breathtaking scenery— upon their return home after two grim weeks of togetherness.

Erma Bombeck

$\mathcal{L}$ots of people have matrimonial troubles and don't know it.

Oliver Herford

$\mathcal{A}$ simple enough pleasure, surely, to have breakfast alone with one's husband, but how seldom married people in the midst of life achieve it.

Anne Morrow Lindbergh

$\mathcal{M}$oreover just as I am unsure of the difference
    between flora and fauna and flotsam and jetsam
I am quite sure that marriage is the alliance of
    two people one of whom never remembers
    birthdays and the other never forgetsam.

Ogden Nash

$\mathcal{N}$o man is a hero to his wife's psychiatrist.

Eric Berne

Of all actions of a man's life, his marriage does least concern other people, yet of all actions of our life, 'tis most meddled with by other people.

John Selden

$\mathcal{P}$eople are always asking couples whose marriage has endured at least a quarter of a century for their secret for success. Actually, it is no secret at all. I am a forgiving woman. Long ago, I forgave my husband for not being Paul Newman.

Erma Bombeck

Wife: A former sweetheart.

H. L. Mencken

The husband was a teetotaller, there was no other woman, and the conduct complained of was that he had drifted into the habit of winding up every meal by taking out his false teeth and hurling them at his wife.

Sir Arthur Conan Doyle

I married beneath me. All women do.

Lady Astor

The men that women marry,
And why they marry them, will always be
A marvel and a mystery to the world.

Henry Wadsworth Longfellow

Every man who is high up loves to think that he has done it all himself; and the wife smiles, and lets it go at that. It's our only joke. Every woman knows that.

J. M. Barrie

Behind every man who achieves success
Stand a mother, a wife and the IRS.

Ethel Jacobson

*N*othing flatters a man as much as the happiness of his wife; he is always proud of himself as the source of it.

Samuel Johnson

*T*he road to success is filled with women pushing their husbands along.

Sir Thomas Robert Dewar

$\mathcal{N}$o man should marry until he has studied anatomy and dissected at least one woman.

Honoré de Balzac

I've been trying to fashion a wifely ideal,
    And find that my tastes are so far from concise
That, to marry completely, no fewer than three'll
    Suffice.

Owen Seaman

$\mathcal{M}$istresses we keep for pleasure, concubines for daily attendance upon our persons, wives to bear us legitimate children and to be our faithful housekeepers.

Demosthenes

Often the difference between a successful marriage and a mediocre one consists of leaving about three or four things a day unsaid.

Harlan Miller

Marriage always demands the greatest understanding of the art of insincerity possible between two human beings.

Vicki Baum

*I*ntelligent discussion of practically everything is what is
breaking up modern marriage.

E. B. White

I do not see how there can be any real respect,
Or any real privacy such as women love,
When you marry a man.
    A man makes trouble.

Josephine Dodge Bacon

I think it can be stated without denial that no man ever saw a man he would be willing to marry if he were a woman.

George Gibbs

*A*ny intelligent woman who reads the marriage contract, and then goes into it, deserves all the consequences.

Isadora Duncan

Marriage: A ceremony in which rings are put on the finger of the lady and through the nose of the gentleman.

Herbert Spencer

*M*arriage is a great institution, but I'm not ready for an institution.

Mae West

*M*arriage: A legal or religious ceremony by which two persons of the opposite sex solemnly agree to harass and spy on each other for ninety-nine years, or until death do them join.

Elbert Hubbard

*B*igamy is having one husband too many. Monogamy is the same.

Erica Jong

A honeymoon is a good deal like a man laying off to take an expensive vacation, and coming back to a different job.

Edgar Watson Howe

*T*here is a lot to get used to in the first year of marriage. One wakes up in the morning and finds a pair of pigtails on the pillow that were not there before.

Martin Luther

*I*t doesn't much signify whom one marries, for one is sure to find next morning that it was someone else.

Samuel Rogers

Comparing one man with another,
You'll find this maxim true.
That the man who is good to his mother
Will always be good to you.

Fred Emerson Brooks

*M*en often marry their mothers.

Edna Ferber

*M*y wife is the kind of girl who'll not go anywhere without her mother, and her mother will go anywhere.

John Barrymore

*D*on't try to marry an entire family or it may work out that way.

George Ade

Marriage is like life in this—that it is a field of battle, and not a bed of roses.

Robert Louis Stevenson

In marriage, as in war, it is permitted to take every advantage of the enemy.

Douglas Jerrold

*M*y wife was too beautiful for words, but not for arguments.

John Barrymore

*T*he only thing that holds a marriage together is the husband being big enough to step back and see where the wife was wrong.

Archie Bunker

*W*edlock, as old men note, hath likened been
Unto a public crowd or common rout;
Where those that are without would fain get in,
And those that are within, would fain get out.

Benjamin Franklin

34

*D*ivorce dates from just about the same time as marriage; I think that marriage is a few weeks older.

Voltaire

*L*ove, the quest; marriage, the conquest; divorce, the inquest.

Helen Rowland

*A*las, she married another; they frequently do; I hope she is happy—because I am.

Artemus Ward

*I*f a man really loves a woman, of course he wouldn't marry her for the world if he were not quite sure that he was the best person she could by any possibility marry.

Oliver Wendell Holmes

"*I* hope I'm doing the right thing" he thought looking in the mirror. "Am I good enough for her?" Roger need not have worried because he was.

John Lennon

A maiden marries to please her parents; a widow to please herself.

Proverb

*I*nstead of marrying "at once," it sometimes happens that we marry "at last."

Colette

Pussy said to the Owl, "You elegant fowl,
    How charmingly sweet you sing!
Oh! let us be married; too long we have tarried:
    But what shall we do for a ring?"
They sailed away, for a year and a day,
    To the land where the bong-tree grows;
And there in the wood a Piggy-wig stood,
    With a ring at the end of his nose,
        His nose,
        His nose,
With a ring at the end of his nose.

"Dear Pig, are you willing to sell for one shilling
    Your ring?" Said the Piggy, "I will."
So they took it away, and were married next day
    By the Turkey who lives on the hill.

Edward Lear

$\mathcal{T}$here's one fool at least in every married couple.

Henry Fielding

$\mathcal{M}$arried life ain't so bad after you get so you can eat the things your wife likes.

Frank McKinney Hubbard

$\mathcal{T}$here is one thing more exasperating than a wife who can cook and won't, and that's the wife who can't cook and will.

Robert Frost

*T*hrough all the years of my marriage, my love for Camille, like my stomach, has steadily grown.

Bill Cosby

*H*usbands are married for better or worse—but not for lunch.

Erma Bombeck

$\mathcal{D}$ear George—

I'm addicted to gambling. I'll bet on anything, and I've lost more money than I can count. I want to have a normal life, settle down and have a family, but I can't stop gambling long enough to do that.

   Crapped Out

Dear Crapped—

Get married. The odds on winning aren't any better. You'll still have a lot of bad nights, but if it doesn't work out, your wife can only get half of what you started with.

   George Burns

Women's total instinct for gambling is satisfied
by marriage.

Gloria Steinem

What they do in Heaven we are ignorant of; what they
do *not* we are told expressly; that they neither marry, nor
are given in marriage.

Jonathan Swift

My advice to girls: first, don't smoke—to excess;
second, don't drink—to excess; third, don't marry
—to excess.

Mark Twain

*I*n matters of religion and matrimony I never give any advice, because I will not have anybody's torments in this world or the next laid to my charge.

Lord Chesterfield

*A*ny man today who returns from work, sinks into a chair, and calls for his pipe is a man with an appetite for danger.

Bill Cosby

*N*o laborer in the world is expected to work for room, board, and love—except the housewife.

Letty Cottin Pogrebin

*N*o wife can endure a gambling husband unless he is a steady winner.

Sir Thomas Robert Dewar

*W*hen billing and cooing results in matrimony, the billing always comes after the cooing.

Tom Masson

$\mathcal{T}$he hardest task of a girl's life is to prove to a man that his intentions are serious.

Helen Rowland

$\mathcal{T}$he world . . . is chock-full of interesting and curious things. The point of the courtship—marriage—is to secure someone with whom you wish to go hand in hand through this source of entertainment, each making discoveries, and then sharing some and merely reporting others.

Judith Martin (Miss Manners)

I should like to see any kind of a man, distinguishable from a gorilla, that some good and even pretty woman could not shape a husband out of.

Oliver Wendell Holmes

$\mathcal{T}$he most happy marriage I can picture or imagine to myself would be the union of a deaf man to a blind woman.

Samuel Coleridge

*Y*ou must come to our house next time. Absolute peace. Neither of us ever says a word to each other. That's the secret of a successful union.

Alan Ayckbourn

*I*t is generally accepted that a man should discuss his wife as little as possible, but not generally understood that he should discuss himself even less.

La Rochefoucauld

*N*ever feel remorse for what you have thought about
your wife; she has thought much worse things about you.

Jean Rostand

I think of my wife, and I think of Lot,
And I think of the lucky break he got.

William Cole

*M*odern women understand everything except their
husbands.

Oscar Wilde

$\mathcal{E}$very man plays the fool once in his life, but to marry is playing the fool all one's life long.

William Congreve

$\mathcal{W}$hen you've had a bad day and need tenderness and understanding does your husband (a) wrap you in his arms and tell you he adores you or (b) read the paper and absentmindedly scratch you behind your ear and call you the dog's name?

Erma Bombeck

$\mathcal{N}$ever go to bed mad. Stay up and fight.

Phyllis Diller

Marriage is love's demi-tasse.

Elbert Hubbard

It [marriage] happens as with cages: the birds without despair to get in, and those within despair of getting out.

Michel de Montaigne

When a woman gets married, it's like jumping i
hole in the ice in the middle of winter: you do it
you remember it the rest of your days.

   Maxim Gorky

I'd like to get married because I like the idea of a man
being required by law to sleep with me every night.

   Carrie Snow

A man and a woman marry because both of them
don't know what to do with themselves.

   Anton Chekhov

*W*omen have been so highly educated that nothing should surprise them except happy marriages.

Oscar Wilde

*D*ear Abby:
What factor do you think is the most essential if a woman is to have a lasting marriage?

Dotty

Dear Dotty:
A lasting husband.

Abigail Van Buren

A small woman always seems newly married.

Proverb

The poor wish to be rich, the rich wish to be hap
the single wish to be married, and the married wish
to be dead.

Ann Landers

There are only three basic jokes, but since the
mother-in-law joke is not a joke but a very serious
question, there are only two.

George Ade

*W*hen mother-in-law comes in at the door, love flies out the window.

Helen Rowland

*U*nder the best of circumstances, reforming a mother-in-law is extremely dangerous and difficult.

Judith Martin (Miss Manners)

*B*e kind to your mother-in-law, and if necessary pay for her board at some good hotel.

Josh Billings

*T*he lover thinks oftener of reaching his mistress than does the husband of guarding his wife; the prisoner thinks oftener of escaping than does the jailer of shutting the door.

Stendhal

*W*hen a man steals your wife, there is no better revenge than to let him keep her.

Sacha Guitry

The chains of marriage are so heavy that it takes two to bear them, and sometimes three.

Alexandre Dumas fils

*A*dultery: Democracy applied to love.

H. L. Mencken

Marriage is really tough because you have to deal with feelings and lawyers.

Richard Pryor

Trust your husband, adore your husband, and get as much as you can in your own name.

Joan Rivers

I was married by a judge. I should have asked for a jury.

George Burns

Marriage is like a bank account. You put it in, you take it out, you lose interest.

Professor Irwin Corey

Wasn't marriage, like life, unstimulating and unprofitable and somewhat empty when too well ordered and protected and guarded? Wasn't it finer, more splendid, more nourishing, when it was, like life itself, a mixture of the sordid and the magnificent; of mud and stars; of earth and flowers; of love and hate and laughter and tears and ugliness and beauty and hurt?

Edna Ferber

Marriage is popular because it combines the maximum of temptation with the maximum of opportunity.

George Bernard Shaw

$\mathcal{B}$righam Young has two hundred wives. . . . He loves not wisely but two hundred well. He is dreadfully married. He's the most married man I ever saw in my life.

Artemus Ward

$\mathcal{P}$olygamy—how much more poetic it is to marry one and love many.

Oscar Wilde

$\mathcal{V}$ariability is one of the virtues of a woman. It obviates the crude requirements of polygamy. If you have one good wife you are sure to have a spiritual harem.

G. K. Chesterton

$\mathcal{B}$igamy is one way of avoiding the painful publicity of divorce and the expense of alimony.

Oliver Herford

$\mathcal{H}$ow men hate waiting while their wives shop for clothes and trinkets; how women hate waiting, often for much of their lives, while their husbands shop for fame and glory.

Thomas Szasz

*I*t takes a man twenty-five years to learn to be married; it's a wonder women have the patience to wait for it.

Clarence B. Kelland

*T*he majority of husbands remind me of an orangutan trying to play the violin.

Honoré de Balzac

A loving wife will do anything for her husband except stop criticizing and trying to improve him.

J. B. Priestley

61

*I*n my conscience I believe the baggage loves me, for she never speaks well of me herself, nor suffers anybody else to rail at me.

William Congreve

A man's friends like him but leave him as he is: his wife loves him and is always trying to turn him into somebody else.

G. K. Chesterton

One can, to an almost laughable degree, infer
what a man's wife is like from his opinions about women
in general.

John Stuart Mill

Commuter—*One who spends his life
in riding to and from his wife;
A man who shaves and takes a train,
And then rides back to shave again.*

E. B. White

*L*iterature is mostly about having sex and not much about having children. Life is the other way round.

David Lodge

*B*are walls make giddy housewives.

Proverb

*T*he great advantage of a hotel is that it's a refuge from home life.

George Bernard Shaw

*M*arriage is part of a sort of '50s revival package that's back in vogue along with neckties and naked ambition.

Calvin Trillin

Wives and children have never been anything but trouble for a president.

Andrew A. Rooney

Men enter local politics solely as a result of being unhappily married.

C. Northcote Parkinson

*I*n marriage, a man becomes slack and selfish, and undergoes a fatty degeneration of his moral being.

Robert Louis Stevenson

*O*f all modern notions, the worst is this: that domesticity is dull. Inside the home, they say, is dead decorum and routine; outside is adventure and variety. But the truth is that the home is the only place of liberty, the only spot on earth where a man can alter arrangements suddenly, make an experiment or indulge in a whim. The home is not the one tame place in a world of adventure; it is the one wild place in a world of rules and set tasks.

G. K. Chesterton

*T*here's a book in every marriage.

Erma Bombeck

Concessions are essential at the outset of marital life, but after a certain lapse of time you can't afford to lose any more ground.

Jean Rostand

All married couples should learn the art of battle as they should learn the art of making love.

Ann Landers

When you see a married couple coming down the street, the one who is two or three steps ahead is the one that's mad.

Helen Rowland

Wedlock: The deep, deep peace of the double bed after the hurly-burly of the chaise longue.

Mrs. Patrick Campbell

*M*arriage. The beginning and the end are wonderful. But the middle part is hell.

Enid Bagnold

*M*arriage: A woman's hair net tangled in a man's spectacles on top of the bedroom dresser.

Don Herold

*M*arriage: A job. Happiness or unhappiness has nothing to do with it.

Kathleen Norris

*I*n recent years it has become common to hear people all over the country speak of long-term marriage in a tone of voice that assumes it to be inextricably intertwined with the music of Lawrence Welk.

Calvin Trillin

*D*id anyone I know have a "meaningful relationship"? My parents stayed together forty years, but that was out of spite.

Woody Allen

Marriage is a mistake of youth—which we should all make.

Don Herold

Marriage is three parts love and seven parts forgiveness of sins.

Langdon Mitchell

Marriage resembles a pair of shears, so joined that they can not be separated; often moving in opposite directions, yet always punishing anyone who comes between them.

Sydney Smith

Marriage involves big compromises all the time. International-level compromises. You're the U.S.A., he's the USSR, and you're talking nuclear warheads.

Bette Midler

'$T$is safest in matrimony to begin with a little aversion.

Richard Brinsley Sheridan

*D*ear Marilyn:
Why are some men so smart, neat, caring, and helpful—
until they become husbands?

Anonymous

Dear Reader:
Probably for the same reason that some women are so smart,
neat, caring, and helpful until they become wives.

Marilyn vos Savant

*I*t's clear what Bob and I both need: a *wife!*

Jane Wagner

*T*he wonderful thing about marriage is that you are the
most important person in someone else's life. If you don't
come home some evening, there is someone who is going
to go out looking for you.

Dr. Joyce Brothers

A husband should always know what is the matter with his wife, for she always knows what is not.

Honoré de Balzac

*M*arriage develops a binocular view of life, both masculine and feminine.

Dr. William Brown

$\mathcal{D}$ear George—

When my husband and I got married I thought we'd be a very happy couple. Now that the honeymoon is over I realize he's not interested in the things I like to do, and I'm not interested in the things he likes to do. Is our marriage doomed?

Working At It

Dear Work—

Not necessarily. The fact that both of you are not interested in things the other one likes proves that you *do* have something in common. And that's a good beginning. Just be careful not to pressure one another into doing something you both like to do.

I suggest you find things neither of you like to do, and spend as much time as possible doing them together. For instance, not watching television together can be most enjoyable. And if you want a good, long, happy marriage, why don't you consider living in different towns together.

George Burns

I'd be crazy to propose to her, but when I see that profile of hers I feel the only thing worth doing in the world is to grab her and start shouting for clergymen and bridesmaids to come running.

P. G. Wodehouse

'*T*is more blessed to give than to receive; for example, wedding presents.

H. L. Mencken

*I*f it were not for the presents, an elopement would be preferable.

George Ade

*I*n all the wedding cake, hope is the sweetest of plums.

Douglas Jerrold

$\mathcal{M}$arriage is our last, best chance to grow up.

Joseph Barth

$\mathcal{B}$ecause the condition of marriage is worldly and its meaning communal, no one party to it can be solely in charge. What you alone think it ought to be, it is not going to be. Where you alone think you want it to go, it is not going to go. It is going where the two of you—and marriage, time, life, history, and the world—will take it.

Wendell Berry

*E*verything in life is fairly simple except one's wife.

Don Herold

*M*arriage is based on the theory that when a man discovers a particular brand of beer exactly to his taste he should at once throw up his job and go to work in the brewery.

George Jean Nathan

I never knew what real happiness was until I got married. And by then it was too late.

Max Kauffmann

A man in love is incomplete until he has married. Then he's finished.

Zsa Zsa Gabor

*N*ever trust a husband too far, nor a bachelor too near.

Helen Rowland

*W*hen a man brings his wife flowers for no reason—
there's a reason.

Molly McGee

*A*lways remember, Peggy, it's matrimonial suicide to be
jealous when you have a really good reason.

Clare Boothe Luce

*M*y husband wanted to live in sin, even *after* we were married.

James Thurber

I began as a passion and ended as a habit, like all husbands.

George Bernard Shaw

*Y*ou and your husband are alone in a cabin for the first time since your marriage. He is nibbling on your ear. Do you (a) nibble back or (b) tell him the toilet is running?

Erma Bombeck

*I*t destroys one's nerves to be amiable every day to the same human being.

Benjamin Disraeli

A sweetheart is a bottle of wine; a wife is a wine bottle.

Charles Baudelaire

*V*enus, a beautiful good-natured lady, was the goddess of love; Juno, a terrible shrew, the goddess of marriage; and they were always mortal enemies.

Jonathan Swift

A lady's imagination is very rapid; it jumps from admiration to love, from love to matrimony in a moment.

Jane Austen

*W*hen a girl marries she exchanges the attentions of many men for the inattention of one.

Helen Rowland

*I*t is better to have loved your wife than never to have loved at all.

Edgar Saltus

Marriage is the best magician there is. In front of your eyes it can change an exciting, cute little dish into a boring dishwasher.

Ryan O'Neal

Twenty years of romance make a woman look like a ruin; but twenty years of marriage make her look like a public building.

Oscar Wilde

My notion of a wife at forty is that a man should be able to change her, like a bank note, for two twenties.

Douglas Jerrold

A married woman's as old as her husband makes her feel.

Sir Arthur Wing Pinero

We sleep in separate rooms, we have dinner apart, we take separate vacations—we're doing everything we can to keep our marriage together.

Rodney Dangerfield

$\mathbb{B}$ut once a male dove finds a mate,
His coos quite suddenly abate.

Richard Armour

When a man opens the car door for his wife, it's either a new car or a new wife.

Prince Philip (consort of Queen Elizabeth II)

"Home, Sweet Home" must surely have been written by a bachelor.

Samuel Butler

The reason husbands and wives do not understand each other is because they belong to different sexes.

Dorothy Dix

The proper basis for marriage is mutual misunderstanding.

Oscar Wilde

Let no one ever say that marriages are made in Heaven; the gods would not commit so great an injustice.

Marguerite of Valois

*I*f married couples did not live together, happy marriages would be more frequent.

Friedrich Nietzsche

A while back I read where Liz Taylor, commenting on one of her earlier marriages, said the common bond between her and her husband was that they wore the same sweater size.

Erma Bombeck

*I*f you are afraid of loneliness, don't marry.

Anton Chekhov

*T*he dearest object to a married man should be his wife but it is not infrequently her clothes.

James M. Bailey

I tended to place my wife under a pedestal.

Woody Allen

*T*he trouble with many married people is that they are trying to get more out of marriage than there is in it.

Elbert Hubbard

*T*here is more of good nature than of good sense at the bottom of most marriages.

Henry David Thoreau

*M*arriage is the only thing that affords a woman the pleasure of company and the perfect sensation of solitude at the same time.

Helen Rowland

$\mathcal{M}$ore belongs to marriage than four bare legs in a bed.

Proverb

$\mathcal{T}$he husband who desires to surprise is often very much surprised himself.

Voltaire

*I*t's as hard to get a man to stay home after you've married him as it was to get him to go home before you married him.

Helen Rowland

*W*here there's marriage without love, there will be love without marriage.

Benjamin Franklin

*H*ow marriage ruins a man! It's as demoralizing as cigarettes, and far more expensive.

Oscar Wilde

*M*arriage is a wonderful invention; but then again so is a bicycle repair kit.

Billy Connolly

*F*rom my observation, marriage turns men to mush and bliss to blahs.

Jeannie Sakol

*I*t's a funny thing that when a man hasn't got anything on earth to worry about, he goes off and gets married.

Robert Frost

*W*hen you're bored with yourself, marry and be bored with someone else.

David Pryce-Jones

The Perfect Husband:

He tells you when you've got on too much
  lipstick,
And helps you with your girdle when your
  hips stick.

Ogden Nash

An ideal wife is one who remains faithful to you but
tries to be just as charming as if she weren't.

Sacha Guitry

*H*er capacity for family affection is extraordinary. When her third husband died, her hair turned quite gold from grief.

Oscar Wilde

*S*ome men think that being married to a woman means merely seeing her in the mornings instead of in the evenings.

Helen Rowland

I don't know why people should feel that because they have married, they may give up all pretense of good manners and treat their partners as an "old shoe."

Emily Post/Elizabeth L. Post

𝒯he only time most women give their orating husbands undivided attention is when the old boys mumble in their sleep.

Wilson Mizner

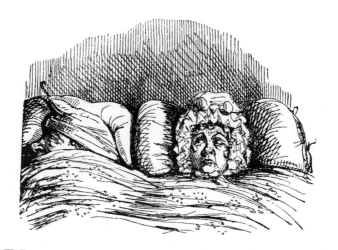

𝒰ncertainty and ambiguity are as exciting in courtship as they are tedious in marriage.

Judith Martin (Miss Manners)

$\mathcal{U}$nmarried men very rarely speak the truth about the things that most nearly concern them; married men, never.

Samuel Butler

$\mathcal{K}$eep your eyes wide open before marriage, half-shut afterwards.

Benjamin Franklin

*S*hutting one's eyes is an art, my dear. I suppose there's no use trying to make you see that—but that's the only way one *can* stay married.

Zoë Akins

*H*e who marries is like the Doge who was wedded to the Adriatic. He knows not what there is in that which he marries: mayhap treasures and pearls, mayhap monsters and tempests await him.

Heinrich Heine

A good marriage is at least 80 percent good luck in finding the right person at the right time. The rest is trust.

Nanette Newman

A successful marriage is an edifice that must be rebuilt every day.

André Maurois

*I*f marriages were made by putting all the men's names into one sack and the women's names into another, and having them taken out by a blindfolded child like lottery numbers, there would be just as high a percentage of happy marriages as we have . . . in England.

George Bernard Shaw

Marriage is a business of taking care of a man and rearing his children. . . . It ain't meant to be no perpetual honeymoon.

Clare Boothe Luce

Love is blind, but marriage restores its sight.

Georg Christoph Lichtenberg

After a few years of marriage a man can look right at a woman without seeing her and a woman can see right through a man without looking at him.

Helen Rowland

*E*very marriage tends to consist of an aristocrat and a peasant, of a teacher and a learner.

John Updike

*M*arriage is like a flourishing garden, alive with rich soil, colorful blooms, delightful fragrances and pleasant surprises—and thorns, beetles, weeds and perhaps a mole.

Nancy McCord

*T*he London season is entirely matrimonial; people are either hunting for husbands or hiding from them.

Oscar Wilde

The plural of spouse is spice.

Christopher Morley

It is a matter of life and death for married people to interrupt each other's stories; for if they did not, they would burst.

Logan Pearsall Smith

Husbands are indeed an
irritating form of life,
And yet through some quirk of
Providence most of them are
really very deeply ensconced in
the affection of their wife.

Ogden Nash

*I*t is a truth universally acknowledged, that a single man in possession of a good fortune, must be in want of a wife.

Jane Austen

*M*aids want nothing but husbands, and when they have them they want everything.

Proverb

A man should be taller, older, heavier, uglier and hoarser than his wife.

Edgar Watson Howe

Marriage has many pains, but celibacy has no pleasures.

Samuel Johnson

It is easier to be a lover than a husband for the simple reason that it is more difficult to be witty every day than to produce the occasional *bon mot*.

Honoré de Balzac

$\mathcal{B}$eing a husband is a whole-time job. That is why so many husbands fail. They cannot give their entire attention to it.

Arnold Bennett

$\mathcal{A}$ good husband is never the first to go to sleep at night or the last to awake in the morning.

Honoré de Balzac

*H*usbands are like fires. They go out when unattended.

Zsa Zsa Gabor

*T*o marry a second time represents the triumph of hope over experience.

Samuel Johnson

Marriage is a good deal like a circus: there is not as much in it as is represented in the advertising.

Edgar Watson Howe

Men marry because they are tired; women because they are curious; both are disappointed.

Oscar Wilde

Love-making is radical, while marriage is conservative.

Eric Hoffer

$\mathcal{T}$he days just prior to marriage are like a snappy introduction to a tedious book.

Wilson Mizner

$\mathcal{M}$arriage is a feast where the grace is sometimes better than the dinner.

Charles Caleb Colton

*M*arriage is a book of which the first chapter is written in poetry and the remaining chapters in prose.

Beverly Nichols

*M*arriage is a meal where the soup is better than the dessert.

Austin O'Malley

The moment a woman marries, some terrible revolution happens in her system; all her good qualities vanish, presto, like eggs out of a conjuror's box. 'Tis true that they appear on the other side of the box, but for the husband they are gone forever.

Edward George Bulwer-Lytton

American women expect to find in their husbands a perfection that English women only hope to find in their butlers.

W. Somerset Maugham

*M*arriage: A souvenir of love.

Helen Rowland

*I*n modern wedlock, too many misplace the key.

Tom Masson

*C*oupling doesn't always have to do with sex. . . . Two
people holding each other up like flying buttresses.
Two people depending on each other and babying each
other and defending each other against the world outside.
Sometimes it was worth all the disadvantages of marriage
just to have that: one friend in an indifferent world.

Erica Jong

*H*usband and wife come to look alike at last.

Oliver Wendell Holmes

*G*ood marriages do exist, but not delectable ones.

La Rochefoucauld

No one who ever married could honestly promise to love his or her husband or wife for the rest of life. It is a ridiculous promise for a clergyman to ask a couple to make under threat of not performing the marriage if they refuse.

Andrew A. Rooney

I have known many single men I should have liked in my life (if it had suited them) for a husband: but very few husbands have I ever wished was mine.

Mary Ann Lamb

*W*eddings are wonderful, but I do think they are a trifle dull for people who are not getting married.

Miss Piggy (as told to Henry Beard)

*I*n olden times sacrifices were made at the altar—a custom which is still continued.

Helen Rowland

*T*he music at a wedding procession always reminds me of the music of soldiers going into battle.

Heinrich Heine

I guess walking slow getting married is because it gives you time to maybe change your mind.

Virginia Cary Hudson

*P*olitics doesn't make strange bedfellows —marriage does.

Groucho Marx

A husband is a man who
two minutes after his head
touches the pillow is snoring
like an overloaded omnibus.

Ogden Nash

*B*efore marriage, a man will lie awake thinking about something you said; after marriage, he'll fall asleep before you finish saying it.

Helen Rowland

*H*usbands are awkward things to deal with; even keeping them in hot water will not make them tender.

Mary Buckley

*O*ne can always recognize women who trust their husbands; they look so thoroughly unhappy.

Oscar Wilde

*T*here is so little difference between husbands you might as well keep the first.

Adela Rogers St. Johns

A husband is what is left of a lover after the nerve has been extracted.

Helen Rowland

*M*en have a much better time of it than women; for one thing they marry later; for another thing they die earlier.

H. L. Mencken

A husband should not insult his wife publicly, at parties. He should insult her in the privacy of the home.

James Thurber

*T*here is only one real tragedy in a woman's life. The fact that the past is always her lover, and her future invariably her husband.

Oscar Wilde

One good Husband is worth two good Wives; for the scarcer things are, the more they're valued.

Benjamin Franklin

Love seems the swiftest, but it is the slowest of all growths. No man or woman really knows what perfect love is until they have been married a quarter of a century.

Mark Twain

One doesn't have to get anywhere in a marriage. It's not a public conveyance.

Iris Murdoch

*I*t is as absurd to say that a man can't love one woman all the time as it is to say that a violinist needs several violins to play the same piece of music.

Honoré de Balzac

*T*he very fact that we make such a to-do over golden weddings indicates our amazement at human endurance. The celebration is more in the nature of a reward for stamina.

Ilka Chase

*I*n the presence of someone who has been married a long time to the same person, a lot of people seem to feel the way they might feel in the presence of a Methodist clergyman or an IRS examiner.

Calvin Trillin

*T*here are two marriages, then, in every marital union, his and hers.

Jessie Shirley Bernard

*T*here is no place like a bed for confidential disclosures between friends. Man and wife, they say, there open the very bottom of their souls to each other; and some old couples often lie and chat over old times till nearly morning.

Herman Melville

*I*n a happy marriage it is the wife who provides the climate, the husband the landscape.

Gerald Brenan

*M*arriage is not just spiritual communion and passionate embraces; marriage is also three-meals-a-day and remembering to carry out the trash.

Dr. Joyce Brothers

A difference of taste in jokes is a great strain on the affections.

George Eliot

*I*f you cannot have your dear husband for a comfort and a delight, for a breadwinner and a crosspatch, for a sofa, chair or a hot-water bottle, one can use him as a Cross to be Borne.

Stevie Smith

Very often the only thing that comes between a charming man and a charming woman is the fact that they are married to each other.

Robert de Flers and Gaston Caillavet

Strong are the couples who resort
More to courtship and less to court.

Ogden Nash

*B*eing married six times shows a degree of optimism over wisdom, but I am incorrigibly optimistic.

Norman Mailer

*T*he people people have for friends
Your common sense appall,
But the people people marry
Are the queerest folk of all.

Charlotte Perkins Gilman

6269248

Christe Mitchell

Fri. 1.00

out side

Innwes